Ph

Don Williams
Bill Gerrity

GL Regal Books A Division of G/L Publications
Glendale, California, U.S.A.

Other good Regal reading:
Philippians, Inductive Bible Study Series
  by Don Williams and Bill Gerrity
The Apostle Paul and Women in the Church
  by Don Williams
The Christian Life: Issues and Answers
  by Gary Maeder with Don Williams
The Bond that Breaks
  by Don Williams
Better Bible Study
  by A. Berkeley Mickelsen and Alvera Mickelsen
Miracles Happen in Group Bible Study
  by Albert J. Wollen

The foreign language publishing of all Regal books is under the direction of *Gospel Literature International* (GLINT), a missionary assistance organization founded in 1961 by Dr. Henrietta C. Mears. Each year *Gospel Literature International* provides financial and technical help for the adaptation, translation and publishing of books and Bible study materials in more than 85 languages for millions of people worldwide.

For more information you are invited to write to *Gospel Literature International*, Glendale, California 91204

Published by Regal Books Division, G/L Publications
Glendale, California 91209
Printed in U.S.A.

Library of Congress Catalog Card Number 79-64290
ISBN 0-8307-0703-4
Second Edition 1979

Previously published as *An Introduction to Inductive Bible Study*

Contents

Introduction

I Love a Mystery

"Darkness chases the light from the sky and the fog begins its surge. Slowly it fills the city air until the streets are drunk with it. Reeling in the stewing air the foghorn belches and the city capitulates to its intruder."

Sound like a good setting for a Bible study? Not quite. How about a scene from a Sherlock Holmes movie? Now that's more like it! But what's Sherlock Holmes doing in a book about Bible study? Elementary, my dear Watson, elementary!

Bible study is like solving a mystery—it requires a two-fold process of observation (seeing the clues) and investigation (putting them together). Like Sherlock on a case, we must come to the Bible to collect the facts and then analyze them. What kind of book are we studying? Who wrote it? Why was it written? What did the author want to accomplish? To whom did he write it? What needs did he have? Why did God include this book in the Bible?

As we read we must see how the clues fit together to give us an understanding of the book we are studying. So if you are excited by mysteries, if you have a spirit of adventure, if you delight in discovering things for yourself—inductive Bible study is for you.

But, fear not. We won't ask you to become a theological Sherlock Holmes overnight. Our focus will be to learn *how to study* at the same time that we learn the content of one of the most engaging books in the Bible, Paul's letter to Philemon.

Learning is not a passive but an active process; and in this book we will learn by doing. As someone said:

> When I hear I forget
> When I see I remember
> When I do I understand.

Our active learning process will be in three major steps: (1) we will first observe the text; (2) then we will question it; and (3) (here we leave Sherlock behind) we will apply the results to our own lives.

OBSERVE THE TEXT

For most of us Bible study has been an immediate dash to application. We read a portion of Scripture and then ask ourselves, "What does that mean to me?" God does speak to each of us in a personal way as we read the Bible, but if that's all we consider when we encounter Scripture, then we're missing a great deal. The Bible was written in a living and real historical context. Through it God intervenes in the tumult of a fallen world. The Holy Spirit inspired ancient men with His eternal truth so that today, nearly two millenniums later, we look to the writings of these men, many of whom were "uneducated," for the very words of life. Since God spoke in history, if we want a deeper understanding of what He says then we need to understand that history and the men whom He inspired. This brings us to our first step in inductive study—observation. The following story will make this clear.

A student of Louis Agassiz at Yale University describes his first encounter with the inductive method in a biology class. Agassiz brought in a tin pan with a small fish in it. The student was to study it without communication with any other student or reading any books about fish. His job was to find out what he could about the fish, *from the fish*. After an hour the student felt finished, but Agassiz left him alone for a week.

QUESTION THE TEXT

Dismayed, but challenged, the student spent 100 hours studying the fish. "I got interested in finding out how the scales went in series, their shape, the form and placement of the teeth, etc." At the end of the week, Agassiz was still dissatisfied with the results. The student said, "In another week of 10 hours a day labor, I had results which astonished myself and satisfied him. I shall never forget the sense of power which this experience brought. I had learned the art of comparing objects."

The experience of this young student aptly characterizes inductive Bible study. Undoubtedly we'll all be amazed simply by what we see is there. But believe me, the Bible is more exciting than Agassiz's fish!

Observation is the seeing and the gathering of all information available to us concerning the book of the Bible to be studied. Our "fish" is a letter full of people, places, and things. Like Agassiz's student we will discover all of this information right from the text itself.

To change the metaphor, this part of inductive study is like getting ready to do a jigsaw puzzle. The first thing we do is lay all of the pieces out on the table. After we've examined each one, we discover how to fit them all together. So, in our study, we collect the historical data from the letter (the pieces) and put the scattered information together (the puzzle). In this we discover the letter's origin and purpose. We ask, "Does this piece fit here?" If so, how does it affect the overall picture? We've gathered our material and now we want to thoroughly investigate it to see what part it plays and its meaning in relationship to the whole.

APPLY THE RESULTS

Finally, when all the facts are in and all the questioning is completed, we face the goal of our work, the "fish" examines us. The facts to be collected are the whereabouts of my life and the questioning to be done is when I allow the Holy Spirit to probe me and to convict me. Bible study is a call. It is a call to comfort and it is a call to confrontation and change. In the Bible we find the good news of God's full provision for our sin. Written there is the account of the Good Shepherd who gives up His life for His sheep. Comforting is the news that we have not been left to our own means. Comforting is the realization that God is in the land and that forgiveness is freely available to all who will come.

And to those who come Jesus promises new life. Jesus gives us the hope that in Him we become new creatures. But the new man is wrought out of the old and this brings confrontation and change. Life with the God of all creation is not static. Daily He confronts us with His values and with His ways and He calls us to be like Him. He asks us to take up the cross and to follow Him. But like the great physician that He is His probe only hurts to heal.

Yes, Bible study is high adventure—you'll be examining and testing the very handiwork of God. But remember, the risk is high, it's your life that will be on the line. And if you're willing, you can be confident that you'll never get up from your desk the same person as you were when you sat down.

Introduction to Philemon

We begin by *reading the letter all the way through.* We need to look at the "whole fish." Sometimes when I read I don't concentrate and my comprehension is poor. To guard against this and to make sure we think through the material as we go, we shall make up a summary sentence or title for each paragraph. This will give us a basic overview of the whole letter.

Since this study guide is based on the *New American Standard Bible* the text is printed here for us. The paragraphs are shorter for more intensive study. Use the space provided in the text and write a title for each paragraph. When you have finished, check your work with mine and see if you agree. If not, why not?

CREATE PARAGRAPH TITLES

1:1,2 Title: _____

 1 *Paul, a prisoner of Christ Jesus, and Timothy our*

brother, to Philemon our beloved brother and fellow-worker,

2 and to Apphia our sister, and to Archippus our fellow-soldier, and to the church in your house:

1:3 Title:_____
3 Grace to you and peace from God our Father and the Lord Jesus Christ.

1:4-7 Title:_____
4 I thank my God always, making mention of you in my prayers,

5 because I hear of your love, and of the faith which you have toward the Lord Jesus, and toward all the saints;

6 and I pray that the fellowship of your faith may become effective through the knowledge of every good thing which is in you for Christ's sake.

7 For I have come to have much joy and comfort in your love, because the hearts of the saints have been refreshed through you, brother.

1:8-14 Title:_____
8 Therefore, though I have enough confidence in Christ to order you to do that which is proper,

9 yet for love's sake I rather appeal to you—since I am such a person as Paul the aged, and now also a prisoner of Christ Jesus—

10 I appeal to you for my child, whom I have begotten in my imprisonment, Onesimus,

11 who formerly was useless to you, but now is useful both to you and to me.

12 And I have sent him back to you in person, that is, sending my very heart;

13 whom I wished to keep with me, that in your

behalf he might minister to me in my imprisonment for the gospel;

14   but without your consent I did not want to do anything, that your goodness should not be as it were by compulsion, but of your own free will.

1:15-20 Title:_____

15   For perhaps he was for this reason parted from you for a while, that you should have him back forever,

16   no longer as a slave, but more than a slave, a beloved brother, especially to me, but how much more to you, both in the flesh and in the Lord.

17   If then you regard me a partner, accept him as you would me.

18   But if he has wronged you in any way, or owes you anything, charge that to my account;

19   I, Paul, am writing this with my own hand, I will repay it (lest I should mention to you that you owe to me even your own self as well).

20   Yes, brother, let me benefit from you in the Lord; refresh my heart in Christ.

1:21,22 Title:_____

21   Having confidence in your obedience, I write to you, since I know that you will do even more than what I say.

22   And at the same time also prepare me a lodging; for I hope that through your prayers I shall be given to you.

1:23,24 Title:_____

23   Epaphras, my fellow-prisoner in Christ Jesus, greets you;

24   as do Mark, Aristarchus, Demas, Luke, my fellow-workers.

1:25 Title: _____

25   *The grace of the Lord Jesus Christ be with your
spirit.*
Note: In 1:1,2, e.g., 1: indicates the chapter and 1,2
indicate the verses. Since there is only one chapter in
Philemon this is obvious. Romans 5:12 means chapter 5,
verse 12.

MY PARAGRAPH TITLES

1:1,2 Paul and Timothy greet Philemon and their fellow Christians

1:3 Paul gives them a blessing of grace and peace

1:4-7 Paul thanks God for Philemon and prays for him

1:8-14 Paul appeals for his new convert, Onesimus,
who is returning to Philemon

1:15-20 Onesimus returns as a brother and Paul accepts
responsibility for him

1:21,22 Paul hopes to join Philemon

1:23,24 Greetings to Philemon from Christians with
Paul

1:25 A benediction from Paul.

While these titles give the overall point of the paragraph, they do not exhaust its content. We will bear
down on this later. Right now we have a general picture
of the letter from a simple reading; our questioning and
specific observation come in our actual study.

THE STRUCTURE OF PHILEMON

1. *Salutation*—(author and recipients). "Paul ... to
Philemon"
2. *Blessing*—"Grace to you and peace"
3. *Prayer of thanksgiving and intercession*—"I thank
my God ... and I pray that"

14

4. *Body*—"Therefore, though I have enough confidence"
5. *Farewell greetings*—"Epaphras, my fellow-prisoner in Christ Jesus, greets you."
6. *Benediction*—"The grace of the Lord Jesus Christ be with your spirit."

This is the standard form of a first-century letter, secular or Christian. Just as we begin a letter today with "Dear Mary," so in the Roman world a letter began with the author's name: "Paul." This was followed by the name of the person or persons to whom he wrote, a blessing, a prayer and then the purpose and substance of the letter. All were concluded by a farewell and benediction.

Compare this with the text of a non-Christian letter from Apion, an Egyptian soldier in the Roman army to his father, Epimachus, written in A.D. 20.

Apion to Epimachus his father and lord, many greetings:	*Paul, a prisoner of Christ Jesus, ... to Philemon our beloved brother and fellow-worker ... Grace to you ...*
Before all things I pray that you are in health, and that you do prosper and fare well continually together ...	*I thank my God always, making mention of you in my prayers ...*
I thank the Lord Serapis that, when I was in peril in the sea, he saved me immediately ...	*and I pray that the fellowship of your faith ...*
I beseech you therefore, my lord father, write unto me a	*Therefore, though I have enough confidence in Christ*

15

little letter firstly of your health, secondly of that of my brother and sister, thirdly that I may do obeisance to your hand ...	*to order you to do that which is proper, yet for love's sake I rather appeal to you ...*
Salute Capito much ... I sent you by Euctemon a little picture of me.	*Epaphras, my fellow-prisoner in Christ Jesus, greets you ...*
Fare you well I pray.	*The grace of the Lord Jesus Christ be with your spirit.*

THE HISTORICAL CONTEXT

Our next task is to reconstruct Paul's situation and Philemon's situation, to establish the historical context out of which Paul wrote.

To do this we shall record everything we can find out about Paul and everything we can find out about Philemon. Here we are interested in historical facts, not general theological ideas. For example, in verse 3 we find that Paul believes in grace and peace "from God our Father and the Lord Jesus Christ." We will not record this here, however, because it does not add to our historical understanding of Paul's specific situation.

Since Onesimus is also important we shall add him, too.

Go back through the letter using the guide below and jot down your historical observations about Paul, Philemon and Onesimus.

I have written in the answers to verse 1 so that you will have a clear idea of what we are talking about. Compare your work with mine on page 18 after you are through.

16

Paul	Philemon	Onesimus
1:1 In prison, Timothy is with him—a brother to Paul and Philemon	1:1 Beloved brother and fellow-worker to Paul and Timothy	
	1:2	
1:5	1:5	
1:7	1:7	
1:8		
1:9		
1:10		1:10
1:11	1:11	1:11
1:12	1:12	1:12
1:13	.1:13	1:13

Paul	Philemon	Onesimus
1:14	1:14	
	1:15	
1:16	1:16	1:16
1:17	1:17	
1:18	1:18	1:18
1:19	1:19	
1:20	1:20	
1:21		
1:22	1:22	
1:23,24		

Paul	Philemon	Onesimus
1:1 In prison, Timothy is with him—a brother to Paul and Philemon	1:1 beloved brother and fellow-worker to Paul and Timothy	

18

Paul	Philemon	Onesimus
	1:2 Apphia, Archippus and the church meet in Philemon's house	
1:5 Paul hears a report about Philemon	1:5 Philemon has love and faith to Christ and all Christians (saints)	
1:7 Paul receives joy and comfort from Philemon's love	1:7 Philemon takes care of the Christians (saints) refreshing them	
1:8 Paul is bold to order Philemon		
1:9 Paul, the aged and a prisoner, prefers to appeal for love's sake		
1:10 Paul appeals for his child Onesimus whom he has converted in jail.		1:10 Onesimus has become a Christian through Paul

19

Paul	Philemon	Onesimus
1:11 Onesimus is useful to Paul	1:11 Onesimus is useful to Philemon	1:11 Onesimus is useful: a changed man
1:12 Paul is returning Onesimus to Philemon with love	1:12 Onesimus came from Philemon	1:12 Onesimus is going back to Philemon
1:13 Paul would have been happy to have had Onesimus's ministry	1:13 If with Paul, Onesimus would have ministered on behalf of Philemon	1:13 Onesimus's ministry to Paul represents Philemon
1:14 Paul wants Philemon's consent, by his own free will	1:14 For Onesimus to stay Paul needs Philemon's consent	
	1:15 Onesimus was parted from Philemon; now he is back forever	
1:16 Paul sees Onesimus as a brother now	1:16 Philemon gets Onesimus back as more than a slave— as a brother	1:16 Onesimus was Philemon's slave

Paul	Philemon	Onesimus
1:17 Paul and Philemon are partners	1:17 Philemon is to receive Onesimus as he would Paul	
1:18 Paul takes responsibility for any wrongs by Onesimus	1:18 Philemon was probably wronged by Onesimus	1:18 Onesimus probably wronged Philemon and owes him things
1:19 Paul writes that he will repay	1:19 Philemon owes Paul his own self	
1:20 Paul wants to benefit from Philemon	1:20 Philemon is a brother	
1:21 Paul trusts Philemon to do more than he says		
1:22 Paul hopes to come to Philemon	1:22 Philemon has a lodging (guest room) and prays for Paul	
1:23,24 Epaphras, Mark, Aristarchus, Demas and Luke are with Paul		

We now have the raw materials for reconstructing the historical setting of the letter. Summarize Paul's situation, Philemon's situation and Onesimus's situation.

Paul

Philemon

Onesimus

Compare your summary with mine.

Paul
    Paul is aged (1:9) and has great authority (1:8). In the course of his travels he converted Philemon (1:19). Tim-

othy was probably with Paul at the time (1:1, "our brother"). Paul and Philemon entered into a partnership in the gospel (1:17), becoming fellow-workers (1:1). Later Paul found himself in prison (1:1 and 1:9) where he led Onesimus, Philemon's slave (1:16), to Christ (1:10). Now Paul is returning Onesimus to Philemon (1:12), appealing to Philemon for love's sake (1:9) to take him back (1:10), no longer as a slave but as a brother (1:16). Paul will repay any damages done by Onesimus (1:19). He hopes soon to be released from prison to join Philemon (1:22). He has others gathered with him (1:23,24) as he writes this letter.

Philemon

Philemon was converted by Paul (1:19). He is a slave owner (1:16) who has a large enough house to hold a church gathering (1:2) and a lodging for Paul (1:22). He appears to be a wealthy businessman who is called a partner (1:17) and a fellow-worker (1:1) by Paul.

Although his slave Onesimus ran away, legally Philemon controls his destiny. He must choose to receive him back (1:12). If Onesimus had stayed with Paul, it would have been on Philemon's behalf (1:13).

Not only is Philemon a slave owner, he is a Christian. He has a ministry in his home (1:2), trusts the saints (1:5), and refreshes them (1:7). Thus he must make his decision about Onesimus in light of Christ (1:16).

Although probably wronged by Onesimus (1:18) Philemon must treat him as a brother (1:16). Paul hopes Philemon's goodness will come freely (1:14).

Onesimus

Onesimus is a slave (1:16) who ran away from Philemon (1:15). Now he has been converted in prison by Paul (1:10). This has issued in a changed life (1:11) and

Paul is returning Onesimus to Philemon (1:12). He comes back as a brother (1:16). When he left he probably wronged Philemon (1:18) but Paul promises to take care of that (1:18,19).

We are now ready to summarize Paul's reason or reasons for writing. What do you think? Put it down.

Paul's Reason(s) for Writing:

Compare your results with mine:

Paul writes to heal a broken relationship. Between Philemon and Onesimus stands Paul, and this letter represents his attempt to bring these two men together as brothers in Christ. Since we live in a world of division and hate today, we can begin to see the importance of this letter to our lives. We, like Paul, must reconcile people in the name of Christ.

Now we are ready to study Paul's letter. We know the historical setting out of which it emerged. We know Paul's goal in writing and are ready to see his strategy and tactics unfold as we observe and question each part of the text.

THE INDUCTIVE QUESTIONS

As we turn to the text itself we will use six questions to uncover its meaning.

24

(1) *The language question deals with vocabulary.* What do the words mean?

This question also deals with *style.* Is it poetry or prose? A letter or proverb or parable? How is it being said? What is the form or sentence structure? Why are the particular words chosen? Where do they appear in the context?

(2) *The historical question deals with the setting of the text and its historical content.* Who is speaking or acting? What is being said of a historical nature? When is it happening? We have already dealt with this question at length in our previous study. This will be just a review.

(3) *The theological question deals with the theological content.* What truths are taught about the nature of God, man, sin, salvation, the church, the Christian life, etc.? How can we understand them systematically?

(4) *The tactical question deals with where a particular paragraph or idea fits in light of Paul's reasons for writing.* We have used a military metaphor to explain this. A commander creates a strategy and uses tactics to form his battle-plan in winning a war. A coach creates a game-plan to use his team effectively with the proper plays to win the game. A cook follows ordered steps in a recipe to reach the goal of the perfect cake. So Paul uses tactics in accomplishing his goal in writing his letter and we want to see *how* he does this—how one idea leads to the next in reaching the goal.

(5) *The contemporary question deals with the application of the text to our world today.* How do we apply what Paul said to government, politics, economics, business, education, the institutional church, the assumptions, values and goals of our society? What is the social application of the text?

(6) *The personal question deals with the application of the text to our own lives today.* How do we apply what Paul

25

said to our own personalities, needs, families, close friends, moral decisions, goals, etc.? This is the question of discipleship; what am I going to do about what I have learned?

In Part I we shall try to apply all of these questions to Philemon. Sometimes one or more of them may not fit. Don't force yourself to write something; meditate on the passage, more may come later. A study sheet is included for each paragraph along with starter questions.

In Part II is my own study and comments. Do your own work first. Then check mine. We shall dialogue together as we create this study. Where you disagree with me, great! Go back to the text again. I have used this study with groups and always learned new things. You have things to teach me. The question *always* is: What does the text say and mean? These inductive questions are to be used to open it up to our careful observation. Come with me now and the fun will begin.

Part I

Inductive Bible Study
of Philemon

Inductive Bible Study
of Philemon

INDUCTIVE QUESTIONS FOR PHILEMON 1:1,2

1 Paul, a prisoner of Christ Jesus, and Timothy our brother, to Philemon our beloved brother and fellow-worker,

2 and to Apphia our sister, and to Archippus our fellow-soldier, and to the church in your house:

Language

What words are unfamiliar to you? Define them or look them up in a dictionary.
What is the style of this paragraph?
What words are repeated?

Historical

What do we learn here about Paul?
What do we learn about Philemon?
What do we learn about the church?

Theological

What does it mean for Paul to call himself a "prisoner"?
What does this tell you about the Christian life?
What does it mean for Philemon to be "beloved"?
Beloved by whom?
What is the nature of the church seen here?

Tactical

In light of Philemon's situation:

Why does Paul call himself a prisoner?

Why does Paul mention Timothy?

Why does Paul address Philemon as he does?

Why does Paul mention the other Christians and the church?

Contemporary

How do we view our fellow-Christians?
What would be the value of a house church today?

Personal

How do I affirm my fellow-Christians?
Do I have a Timothy in my life?

INDUCTIVE QUESTIONS FOR PHILEMON 1:3

3   *Grace to you and peace from God our Father and the Lord Jesus Christ.*

Language

How do you define *grace*?
How do you define *peace*?
What is the style of this verse?

Historical

Theological

What does it mean to call God "Father"?
What is Christ's position in relation to what the Father does?
What does it mean to call Christ "Lord"?

32

Tactical

What is the foundation upon which Paul will reconcile Philemon and Onesimus?

Contemporary

What do "grace and peace" mean to people today?

Personal

How do "grace and peace" operate in me?

4   *I thank my God always, making mention of you in my prayers,*

5   *because I hear of your love, and of the faith which you have toward the Lord Jesus, and toward all the saints;*

6   *and I pray that the fellowship of your faith may become effective through the knowledge of every good thing which is in you for Christ's sake.*

7   *For I have come to have much joy and comfort in your love, because the hearts of the saints have been refreshed through you, brother.*

Language

How do you define: *love, faith, joy* and *saints*?
What is the structure of this prayer?

Historical

What do we learn of Paul here?
What do we learn of Philemon?

Theological

What are the functions of love and faith in the Christian life?

Tactical

How does this prayer help to prepare Philemon for Paul's appeal?

What aspects of Philemon's Christian character here would be important in reconciling him to Onesimus?

Contemporary

How should we evaluate Christian ministry today in light of this prayer?

Personal

How do I pray for other Christians?

How does my life affect those around me?

INDUCTIVE QUESTIONS FOR PHILEMON 1:8-14

8 Therefore, though I have enough confidence in Christ to order you to do that which is proper,

9 yet for love's sake I rather appeal to you—since I am such a person as Paul the aged, and now also a prisoner of Christ Jesus—

10 I appeal to you for my child, whom I have begotten in my imprisonment, Onesimus,

11 who formerly was useless to you, but now is useful both to you and to me.

12 And I have sent him back to you in person, that is, sending my very heart;

13 whom I wished to keep with me, that in your behalf he might minister to me in my imprisonment for the gospel;

14 but without your consent I did not want to do anything, that your goodness should not be as it were by compulsion, but of your own free will.

Language

How do you define: *child, begotten, minister?*
How does the style in 1:8,9 reveal that Paul is getting to the point of his letter?

Historical

What do we learn about Paul?
What do we learn about Onesimus?
What do we learn about Philemon?

Theological

What do we learn of the Christian life by Paul's refusal to order Philemon to do what is proper?
What do we see here about Paul's theology of evangelism?

Tactical

What is the nature of Paul's appeal so that Philemon will take Onesimus back?

Contemporary

How does the world seek to heal broken relationships?

How does the gospel heal broken relationships?

Personal

How much am I willing to give up my rights for "love's sake"?

How willing am I to invest my life in new Christians?

15   For perhaps he was for this reason parted from you for a while, that you should have him back forever,

16   no longer as a slave, but more than a slave, a beloved brother, especially to me, but how much more to you, both in the flesh and in the Lord.

17   If then you regard me a partner, accept him as you would me.

18   But if he has wronged you in any way, or owes you anything, charge that to my account;

19   I, Paul, am writing this with my own hand, I will repay it (lest I should mention to you that you owe to me even your own self as well).

20   Yes, brother, let me benefit from you in the Lord; refresh my heart in Christ.

Language

What kind of language does Paul use here to appeal to Philemon?

Why does Paul write in his own hand in 1:19?

Historical

What do we learn about Onesimus here?
What do we learn about Paul here?
What do we learn about Philemon here?

Theological

What does Paul see going on behind the tragic circumstances of Onesimus's running away?
What are the results of Onesimus's conversion?
What does it mean to be a brother "both in the flesh and in the Lord" (1:16)?

Tactical

How does this paragraph conclude Paul's argument for Philemon to take Onesimus back?

Contemporary

What is shown here to be the church's social responsibility to the world?

How is our divided church and culture addressed here?

Personal

How can I bring people together in Christ?

What is the risk for me in seeking to heal broken relationships?

21 Having confidence in your obedience, I write to you, since I know that you will do even more than what I say.

22 And at the same time also prepare me a lodging; for I hope that through your prayers I shall be given to you.

Language

How do you understand Paul's use of "obedience" in 1:21 in light of 1:8,9?

Historical

What more do we learn here about Philemon?

Theological

What is the meaning of Paul's call for obedience?

Tactical

How would this paragraph strengthen Paul's hope for reconciliation?

Contemporary

How can what we say be seen in what we do?

Personal

Where does my Christian life become costly?

23 Epaphras, my fellow-prisoner in Christ Jesus, greets you;

24 as do Mark, Aristarchus, Demas, Luke, my fellow-workers.

Language
What do the titles mean here?

Historical
What do we learn here of Paul's prison life?

Theological

Tactical

What is the value of including these men in the letter in accomplishing Paul's purpose?

Contemporary

What do the titles Paul uses say to the modern church?

Personal

What does all this say to my style of ministry?

INDUCTIVE QUESTIONS FOR PHILEMON 1:25
The grace of the Lord Jesus Christ be with your spirit.

Language
What is the style here?

Historical

Theological
What do we learn about grace?

Tactical

Contemporary
Where will the world see grace?

Personal
What final word does Paul have for me?

Part II

Commentary on Philemon

INDUCTIVE QUESTIONS FOR PHILEMON 1:1,2

1 Paul, a prisoner of Christ Jesus, and Timothy our brother, to Philemon our beloved brother and fellow-worker,

2 and to Apphia our sister, and to Archippus our fellow-soldier, and to the church in your house:

Language

a. *Vocabulary: brother*— a title for a man who belongs to the Christian family; *fellow-worker*—one who works alongside, a term of equality; *sister*—a title for a woman who belongs to the Christian family; *fellow-soldier*—a military metaphor for the Christian life, a term of equality.

b. *Style:* The structure of these verses follows the salu-

tation of the first century letter, "Paul . . . to Philemon." Note the four appearances of the possessive
pronoun "our." Christians belong to one another.

Historical

Paul is in prison. Timothy is with him but probably
not under arrest, otherwise Paul would have written,
"Paul and Timothy, prisoners," Timothy is a brother to
Paul and Philemon and thus is included in the salutation. Philemon is a beloved co-worker to Paul, suggesting a partnership.

Apphia and Archippus are singled out from the
church meeting in Philemon's home, probably because
they live in the house as Philemon's wife and son. Philemon is rich enough to have a house big enough to hold
a church gathering. The house-church is the basic unit
of New Testament Christianity.

Theological

Paul defines himself as a prisoner. This could be a
metaphor for the Christian life or a historical reality.
The context shows us Philemon is "beloved" which
means he is an object of the grace of God. The church
is not a building but a fellowship of people "called out,"
which meets in a house.

In the titles here, especially of the family, we learn a
secret of the early church: they cared for each other and
were committed to each other as brothers and sisters
should be today. To belong to Christ is to belong to
God's family.

Tactical

Paul begins, not by stressing his apostolic authority
but, on his knees. Since he will appeal to Philemon "for
love's sake" (1:9), he does not begin by calling upon him

to salute, but in a humble way, "a prisoner of Christ Jesus."

By mentioning Timothy, whom Philemon knows, Paul strengthens his hand. Timothy concurs with Paul in all that is written.

Philemon is "our beloved brother and fellow-worker," Paul compliments him, builds him up, stressing the warm relationship which they share. This is a necessary preparation for his request. The term fellow-worker stresses Paul's and Philemon's equality.

Apphia and Archippus and the church are all included in the address on the letter. This brings the pressure of the Christian community to bear on the issue at hand. Philemon has to make his decision about Onesimus in light of his fellow Christians; they are calling him into accountability.

Contemporary

Questions for the institutional church: Do we view our fellow Christians as brothers and sisters?

Is the Christian community a real family or a dressed-up group of individuals performing for each other, doing "religious" things?

What is the quality of our Christian fellowship today?

What of the house-church?

Is there a lasting spiritual principle here?

Do we all need to belong to a small group, a church in miniature, where people are known and loved deeply and share real joys and sorrows?

Personal

Too often I lean on my authority in dealing with others. When I do move from humility, from weakness, then things happen. Also I take my fellow-Christians for granted. I rarely compliment and affirm them; I just expect them to be fellow-workers or fellow-soldiers of mine. Paul had Timothy with him. I need a brother Timothy with me. I can't live the Christian life on my own. Do I call upon the Christian community when I make moral decisions? How often my decisions would have been different if my brothers and sisters had been with me.

3   *Grace to you and peace from God our Father and the Lord Jesus Christ.*

Language

a. *Vocabulary:* A standard apostolic blessing including a Christianized form of the Roman greeting "hail" which is here "grace" and the Jewish greeting "peace." Grace is God's unmerited acceptance. Peace is wholeness.

b. *Style:* A blessing, given in God's name.

Historical

Theological

Grace and peace find their source in God our Father and the Lord Jesus Christ. God as Father is the ground of the Christian fellowship as a family. In the Lord's prayer we are taught to call God, "Father." He is the source of our life. What a term of belonging! Now Jesus Christ stands with the Father, He stands on the side of God, both together giving us grace and peace. Jesus does what God does. Here are the raw materials for the deity of Christ. As Lord, Jesus now reigns "at the right hand of the Father." Paul mediates this grace and peace to his church family.

Tactical

The gospel of salvation is the basis and continuing reality of all that Paul seeks to accomplish.

Contemporary

Acceptance and wholeness are not merely psychological realities, they are theological realities with psychological consequences. Our culture is looking for "grace and peace," but looking in the wrong place. Or is it that we Christians have kept hidden where acceptance and wholeness are to be found? Do our fortress-looking churches and our grey lives allure people to "grace and peace"?

Personal

I must check myself out on this. Grace—acceptance. Do I feel it from the Father and the Son? Do I give it to my brothers? How often I am judgmental and defensive. Grace will free me and open me to others. Maybe I do not let my "brother Paul" become the channel of grace to me. Am I too proud for this?

Peace—wholeness. But so often my life is divided. Sin sneaks in, doubt and fear arise, anxiety dogs me. Yet there is Christ sleeping in my stormy boat. "Peace be still"—suddenly the waves and my heart are calmed. If I dare receive it, I must give it. Who needs grace and peace from me this week?

4 *I thank my God always, making mention of you in my prayers,*

5 *because I hear of your love, and of the faith which you have toward the Lord Jesus, and toward all the saints;*

6 *and I pray that the fellowship of your faith may become effective through the knowledge of every good thing which is in you for Christ's sake.*

7 *For I have come to have much joy and comfort in your love, because the hearts of the saints have been refreshed through you, brother.*

Language

a. *Vocabulary: love*—self-giving concern; *faith*—trust; *joy*—gladness at the execution of a ministry encouraged by Paul; *saints*—Christians set apart from the world by God's call.

b. *Style:* Paul employs the prayer of thanksgiving and intercession, common to first-century letters, to communicate his warmth and hope to Philemon.

Historical

Paul has received a report about Philemon's love and faith (1:5) which leads him to thanksgiving. He previously has been comforted by Philemon's love and service to the saints (1:7). Philemon's strong Christian character emerges here, as well as Paul's warm emotional ties to him.

Theological

Paul thanks God for Philemon's love and faith. In so doing he highlights two essential aspects of Christian character. Philemon, "beloved" by God (1:1), reflects that love generally in 1:5 and specifically to Paul and in service to other Christians in 1:7. Philemon's love is active love, refreshing the hearts of the saints. At the same time, Philemon is a man of faith. The double objects of his faith, or better "trust," are the Lord Jesus and all the saints (1:5). As in the case of love, so now in faith or trust, there are both the divine and human dimensions. Here, we are at the heart of the new life in Christ.

Tactical

Having gathered the Christian community in 1:1,2, Paul continues to build a bridge to Philemon. He compliments him and affirms him before appealing to him. After making him safe, the Apostle can give his request. This is good psychology!

Paul stresses love and trust—two elements which are essential if Onesimus is to be welcomed home. Philemon's trust is "toward the Lord Jesus, and toward *all* the saints" (1:5). Paul will soon introduce him to another saint he wants him to trust.

Paul prays that the fellowship of Philemon's faith will become effective "through the knowledge of every good thing." Again, Onesimus will benefit directly from this. Then Paul reminds Philemon of the joy and comfort which has come to him through his service to the saints. Paul is sending him another saint to serve.

Throughout this prayer, then, Paul stresses the very aspects of Philemon's Christian character which must operate in order to receive Onesimus back. Paul affirms and strengthens these traits and then calls Philemon to a new step. At the same time Paul stresses his deep ties to Philemon. If he acts as Paul hopes, it will be partially on the basis of those ties.

Contemporary

How important it is for love and faith to go into action, displaying the reality of Christ in the world. The benefits of the Christian community are seen immediately in Philemon's life. We do not hear of Philemon's being an elder or trustee in the church. We do not hear of his even being a Sunday School teacher or planning an evangelistic crusade. We do hear of his trusting Christ and serving Christians. How simple and central the early Christians were. Why have we gone astray?

Personal

Paul prays for his converts and he prays big prayers. How selfish and trivial my prayers seem in comparison. When did I last pray for a brother's or sister's faith becoming effective through knowing every good thing within for Christ's sake?

Philemon's faith and love give Paul joy and comfort. How rarely do I realize that my Christian life immediately affects those around me. I either change my environment or capitulate to it. When I am discouraged, unbelieving and selfish, others are hurt by it. There is no private sin in the Body of Christ. Do I, like Philemon, refresh the hearts of the saints? God wants me to be a cold mountain spring for thirsty hikers on a hot day. Too often I am a lukewarm, fizzed out soda. May God give me that refreshing water!

8   *Therefore, though I have enough confidence in Christ to order you to do that which is proper,*

9   *yet for love's sake I rather appeal to you—since I am such a person as Paul the aged, and now also a prisoner of Christ Jesus—*

10   *I appeal to you for my child, whom I have begotten in my imprisonment, Onesimus,*

11   *who formerly was useless to you, but now is useful both to you and to me.*

12   *And I have sent him back to you in person, that is, sending my very heart;*

13   *whom I wished to keep with me, that in your behalf he might minister to me in my imprisonment for the gospel;*

14   *but without your consent I did not want to do anything, that your goodness should not be as it were by compulsion, but of your own free will.*

Language

a. *Vocabulary:* child—spiritual son; *Onesimus*—"useful" in the original Greek. This explains the word play in 1:11, "useless" has become "useful"; *father*—spiritual source of life in leading another to Christ.

b. *Style:* Paul comes now to the body of the letter which is his appeal on behalf of Onesimus. Notice how the Apostle stresses his authority as he comes to the point. "Paul the aged, and now also a prisoner of Christ Jesus—I appeal to you." By the whole construction of 1:8-10, its language of authority and appeal and the labored way in which Paul reaches his point, we feel the crisis nature of his request.

Historical

Paul has no doubt about his apostolic authority. He is

61

an "old man" for Christ Jesus and now a prisoner also. Being a prisoner is not just a symbol for Paul's service to Christ because of the time word "now"; he is an old man, but *now* a prisoner. While in prison Paul has converted Onesimus and has strong affection for him. Paul, however, is returning him to Philemon who has authority over him. If Onesimus had stayed with Paul he, legally, would have served Paul on Philemon's behalf. Thus Paul needs Philemon's consent to keep him.

Theological

We see Paul struggle here with acting out the Christian life in love not law. He could command, yet for love's sake he appeals. By appealing he allows Philemon to be a man, to accept the maturity of making his own decision. By appealing he keeps their relationship in the context of love which fulfills the law.

Paul continues his evangelistic ministry in prison—he is not a prisoner of his adverse circumstances. Paul teaches a conversionist theology—he brings a runaway slave to life in Christ but doesn't leave him there. He accepts responsibility as a spiritual father, cares for his new child in the faith, and invests his life into him. The results are remarkable—a changed man. Paul expects the gospel to produce observed behavioral change.

Tactical

As Paul gets to the point he reminds Philemon that he could command (Paul is not wishy-washy about his authority) but prefers to appeal. In so doing he humbles himself and presents the case for Onesimus, the runaway slave. Paul's appeal is:

a. *Evangelical*—Onesimus has been converted. Paul would not attempt to reconcile a broken relationship on any other basis. This goes to the depths of the gospel. We are to be reconciled because God has reconciled us. Only a change in the core of one's being can bring a permanent change in relationships.

b. *Practical*—Onesimus is living a new life. Paul knows Philemon is a pragmatic businessman, interested in what works. The Apostle does not stress Onesimus's conversion, he does stress his changed life. He is useful. He is serving Paul, and in sending him back to Philemon he is sending his very heart. Thus on the basis of his conversion and useful life Paul asks Philemon to take Onesimus back.

Contemporary

We live in a legalistic world where people behave by law, not love. The result is fear and guilt, not the freedom to be what we want to be and what God wants us to be. Paul walks the thin line of love here and trusts it for results. When were we last appealed to, to help or give "for love's sake"? Paul sees the reconciliation of broken relationships only on the evangelical basis of conversion to Christ. Why? Because only Christ delivers us from our selfishness.

The world seeks for political solutions to its brokenness, a new balance of power or terror. What a time for the Christian to probe the shallowness and transitoriness of those solutions.

People seek personal reconciliation on the psychiatrist's couch. While many are delivered from binding emotional problems, there is no lasting reunion apart from reunion with Christ, the source of life.

Paul doesn't play favorites. While he cares about Philemon, a wealthy businessman, he cares just as much for Onesimus, a runaway slave. Here is the universality of the gospel. When will the church break out of its limited class and race orientation? The world waits to see it.

Personal

How much do I manipulate people to do what I want? How much do I set them free, for love's sake, to do what Christ wants? Am I willing to give up my rights "for love's sake"? These are hard questions. Paul invested his life in a slave. No hit and run evangelism here. Do I follow up on new Christians in the same way, or do I give them a booklet on the Christian life and cop out "just trusting the Holy Spirit"?

How emotionally involved do I get with people so that they *know* I love them? Or do I let that just be a theological assumption in our relationship? Do I dare write, "I am sending him back to you, sending my very heart"? How much do I really expect to see changed lives about me? How much do I really expect my own life to change? So often I resign myself to evil. So often I resign myself to the evil in my own heart. Lord, give me a new name—"Useful" for you and your world.

INDUCTIVE QUESTIONS FOR PHILEMON 1:15-20

15 For perhaps he was for this reason parted from you for a while, that you should have him back forever,

16 no longer as a slave, but more than a slave, a beloved brother, especially to me, but how much more to you, both in the flesh and in the Lord.

17 If then you regard me a partner, accept him as you would me.

18 But if he has wronged you in any way, or owes you anything, charge that to my account;

19 I, Paul, am writing this with my own hand, I will repay it (lest I should mention to you that you owe to me even your own self as well).

20 Yes, brother, let me benefit from you in the Lord; refresh my heart in Christ.

Language

Style—The personal narrative continues. Paul communicates to Philemon on his ground using business language: "partner" (1:17) and "charge that to my account" (1:18). In 1:19 Paul, who has undoubtedly been dictating the letter up to this point, picks up the pen and writes himself, as if to sign the receipt, "I, Paul, am writing this with my own hand, I will repay it."

Historical

The situation of Onesimus now emerges with clarity. As a slave, he was under the full authority of Philemon (1:16). Paul still honors this (1:13,14). It is likely that in running away, Onesimus took money or valuables to aid him in his travels (1:18). Now in returning he comes as a Christian brother (1:16), and as such Paul is willing to accept responsibility for any wrong which he has done to Philemon (1:18). Incidentally, Paul reveals that Philemon owes his own self to Paul, probably because the

Apostle was instrumental in his conversion too (1:19).

Theological

Perhaps "he was ... parted" in 1:15 suggests by the passive verb that God's providence was moving behind the tragedy of Onesimus's running away. Note that Paul is suggestive here, not dogmatic. Onesimus's conversion gives him new dignity as a child of God for he goes home "no longer as a slave, but more than a slave, a beloved brother" (1:16). Here is the power of the gospel to (1) establish a new self-image, (2) transcend circumstances, and (3) reconcile broken relationships. While Paul does not abolish slavery here, he abolishes the value system upon which slavery rests—this is the true revolution. Onesimus is now a brother "both in the flesh and in the Lord." In the flesh means physically or personally.

It is possible that Onesimus, a physical brother to Philemon, had sold himself into slavery. More likely, Paul calls him Philemon's brother "in the flesh" as well as "in the Lord" to keep Philemon from spiritualizing his relationship to Onesimus ("we will be in heaven together") and then handing out a severe punishment. Philemon is forced to deal with Onesimus as a whole man, physically and spiritually, and as a whole man he is now a Christian.

Tactical

Paul continues his appeal (1:10). We have seen its evangelical and practical aspects. Now he turns to the theological dimension, suggesting that if Philemon has the eyes to see it, behind the tragedy of Onesimus's flight the providential hand of God was bringing him glory. God does not relieve us of tragedy; He works within it to accomplish His greater purpose. The death

66

of Jesus is our touchstone in understanding this truth. So Onesimus now returns "no longer as a slave, but more than a slave, a beloved brother" (1:16). He left as a frightened, hunted fugitive, he returns as a child of God. By the results, in retrospect, Philemon must see the greatness of God's working. Similarly Joseph said to his brothers after they sold him into slavery in Egypt: "As for you, you meant evil against me, but God meant it for good" (Gen. 50:20).

Having given the theological aspect of his appeal, Paul then turns to the personal in 1:17: "If then you regard me a partner, accept him as you would me." Since Onesimus is the Apostle's spiritual child, he is now an extension of himself as he was an extension of Philemon legally as a slave. Paul accepts responsibility for any of his child's wrongs (1:18). However, Philemon has refreshed the saints (1:7); now he has an opportunity to refresh Paul (1:20).

Contemporary

Paul raises here the whole biblical understanding of history. The clue is death and resurrection. In the midst of the brokenness of world history God brings about His saving history. The world can never understand this, it simply sees the brokenness. The risen Jesus appeared only to His friends. The resurrection is a real event in history but the skeptic will always explain it away psychologically or sociologically. Yet the offense lingers: a runaway slave is going home freely. How do you explain it? Paul refuses to allow Philemon to accept Onesimus as a brother "in the Lord" and not "in the flesh."

When will the church accept rich and poor, black and white, young and old as brothers "in the flesh and in the Lord"? Eleven o'clock on Sunday morning is still the most segregated hour in our nation. What an offense to the gospel. If Onesimus and Philemon were not reunited *physically* then the message of reconciliation would be separated from the ministry of reconciliation and the gospel would degenerate into hopeless idealism or mythology. Paul demands a "two-legged gospel" (Lloyd Ogilvie), personal change with social concern. The two must never be separated again.

Personal

The demand here for me, like Paul, is to bring people together in Christ. It is easy out of my insecurities, my need to be well-liked, my fear of controversy or my fear of losing people's financial support not to confront issues squarely. If I were Paul, I could keep Onesimus with me and write Philemon, telling him how I know he rejoices with me that his slave is a Christian and how I know he would want Onesimus to serve me and grow under my direction, etc. But to send him home, that is something else! Now I have to deal with people directly, now I may get hurt. Shall I send this runaway boy home to his parents? Shall I go with him? Shall I mediate between them? "But Lord, this will cost me time and money and risk. It may not even work. Give me the grace to live reconciliation, not just preach it."

INDUCTIVE QUESTIONS FOR PHILEMON 1:21,22

21   Having confidence in your obedience, I write to you, since I know that you will do even more than what I say.

22   And at the same time also prepare me a lodging; for I hope that through your prayers I shall be given to you.

Language

Vocabulary—obedience in 1:21 apparently contradicts 1:8,9, "though I have enough confidence in Christ to order you . . . yet for love's sake I rather appeal to you." Does Paul end up, in effect, commanding? (Compare also 1:13,14.)

Historical

More evidence is given here for Paul's knowledge of Philemon. He knows his house has a lodging, probably because he stayed there before. This also suggests that Philemon is a wealthy man with a large house and estate.

Theological

The issue of "obedience" is obedience to whom? If it is Paul, then the contradiction stands. If it is to the Lord, then there is no contradiction. Paul appeals so that Philemon might do God's will for love's sake. I prefer the second sense, otherwise 1:21 harshly contradicts the rest of the letter.

Tactical

The personal aspect of the appeal continues. Paul is confident that Philemon will go beyond him in forgiveness and generosity. Just to make sure, he plans an early visit to Philemon upon his release. There is no pressure like presence. That Paul would go to Philemon shows how crucial he feels this matter to be.

Contemporary

The world and the church demand that we back up what we say by what we do. Here is the great struggle, but the gospel must be seen. We must visit those whom we address. Christ will be seen *in us*.

Personal

Am I willing to back my requests with my time, effort, energy and *presence*—at cost to my personal life? "This Christian life is hard, Lord. I guess you lived this way; you will have to live this way again in me."

23 Epaphras, my fellow-prisoner in Christ Jesus, greets you;

24 as do Mark, Aristarchus, Demas, Luke, my fellow-workers.

Language

a. *Vocabulary: fellow-prisoner* and *fellow-workers*, like "fellow-worker" and "fellow-soldier" in 1:1,2, are terms of equality. Paul draws others alongside himself in a shared ministry.

b. *Style:* Farewell greetings.

Historical

Epaphras seems also to be under arrest with Paul since he is spoken of as a "fellow-prisoner" in distinction to the rest in 1:24. Paul also has several other companions with him. His imprisonment must be quite open and flexible.

Theological

Tactical

Other Christians are drawn into the letter creating further pressure from a wide consensus as to the rightness of Paul's request to Philemon.

Contemporary

Does the church offer a shared ministry or a hierarchical ministry of status, roles, symbols and degrees of authority?

Personal

"Lord, help me to draw my fellow-workers about me and honor them. Let me reflect on my need for affirma-

71

tion and give it away to others. Make me appreciative of simple, faithful Christians. Crucify my star qualities. Get me back to feet-washing. Let me begin by letting you wash my feet. Break me, Lord, your way with your love."

INDUCTIVE QUESTIONS FOR PHILEMON 1:25

25   The grace of the Lord Jesus Christ be with your spirit.

Language
Style—A standard benediction. See 1:3.

Historical

Theological
Grace is Christ's possession and gift to us. It comes through His Spirit to our spirit.

Tactical

Contemporary
Where will the world see grace? Only by looking at Jesus. How often our needs are misdirected to the wrong place. Grace is *in* Jesus. Here it comes *through* Paul's prayer. But let us look not to the means but the source: Jesus.

Personal
Do I minister Christ's grace to those about me? Am I the means and channel of His grace? "Lord, who is sufficient for these things? Only you." I too am driven back to the source. "Thou hast made us for thyself, and our hearts are restless until they find rest in thee" (Augustine).

IN CONCLUSION

We have learned to study Philemon inductively by observing and questioning the text. We see that the letter is an organic whole, dominated by Paul's desire to reconcile Onesimus and Philemon. This goal determines the content and movement of the letter. The Apostle uses the salutation and prayer to further his goal. The body of the letter contains an appeal in four aspects: evangelical, practical, theological, and personal.

We see through the letter some major points emerging:

1. Paul's desire to work out his relationship with Philemon through love, not law.

2. Paul's demand that the gospel of reconciliation be seen as well as heard.

3. The evangelical basis of reconciliation.

4. The universality of the gospel touching the top and bottom of Roman society: a wealthy businessman and a runaway slave.

5. The undercutting of slavery by Paul's challenge to its value system.

6. The warmth of Paul's relationships with Philemon and Onesimus and his ability to share this freely.

7. Paul's sense of the providence of God.

8. Paul's willingness to accept responsibility for his converts.

Some have seen in this letter Paul writing with a velvet glove hiding a mailed fist. It does not appear that the Apostle leaves Philemon any outs. While this is true, it is understandable and necessary in light of slavery in the first century. The slave is property and the owner has total sovereignty over him. Many runaway slaves were tortured, maimed and even executed upon their return as examples to the others. Paul could not leave this matter to chance.

What emerges from Philemon is a beautiful picture of how the gospel was changing the Roman Empire in the first century. A runaway slave gets on a ship and sails home. There are no chains. There is no guard. He is returning freely. All he has is a little letter in his hand and new life in his heart. This is what Jesus Christ was and is still doing.

Did Philemon take Onesimus back? Most certainly so. This letter was not destined for the scrap pile, but lovingly copied, shared and transmitted until it found its way into our Bible. Why? Because it expressed a new life and a new hope treasured in the early church as both Philemon and Onesimus were treasured brothers in Christ. "The grace of the Lord Jesus Christ be with your spirit" (Philemon 1:25).

FURTHER THINGS TO DO

1. Make an exhaustive outline of Philemon.
   Example: 1:1-3
   I. Salutation
      A. Paul—author
         1. In prison for Christ
         2. Accompanied by brother Timothy
      B. Philemon—recipient
         1. Brother of Timothy
         2. Beloved fellow-worker of Paul and Timothy
      C. Others who share the letter
         1. Apphia—sister
         2. Archippus—fellow-soldier
         3. Church in Philemon's house
   II. Blessing
      A. Grace and Peace
         1. Object—"you"
         2. Source—God our Father and the Lord Jesus Christ

2. Rewrite Paul's letter to Philemon in your own contemporary language. For example: "Paul, busted for Christ Jesus, and Timothy our Christian brother. To Philemon, whom we and God love a lot as he works by our side, and Apphia, our Christian sister, and Archippus who is in the battle with us, and the body of Christians around you . . . "

Part III

Studies for Individuals and Small Groups

Studies for Individuals and Small Groups

STUDY I—PHILEMON:
AN EXAMPLE OF LOVE AND FAITH

1. Pray for God to give you an open heart for this study.
2. Read verses 1-7 in Philemon.
3. Look back at verses 4-7 and give immediate answers to these questions.
   a. Is there anything here that you don't understand? What needs clarification?
   b. What's your first impression of the type of man Philemon is?
   c. What new insights or thoughts strike you?
4. Describe Philemon.
   a. What are his qualities that Paul points out?
   b. What are some ways that Philemon might have expressed these qualities?
   c. For what does Paul pray?
5. Respond personally to what you see.

a. Do you know of anyone today who is like Philemon as described in 4-7? Describe them.

b. How might you become more like Philemon?

c. What does it mean to have faith toward all the saints?

6. A thought to ponder: If someone were to say this about you how would he fill in the blank, "I thank my God always when I remember you in my prayers, because _____."

STUDY II—TO OBEY OR NOT TO OBEY:
THAT IS THE QUESTION

1. Pray that God will give you a clear mind and a willing heart for this study.

2. Read Philemon 8-14 and give immediate answers to the questions without a lot of pondering.

a. Is there anything here that you don't understand? What needs clarification?

b. What is Paul's point here?

c. What new insights or thoughts strike you?

3. Recreate the situation.

a. Where is Paul? Who is he with? Why is he there?

b. Where is Philemon? Who is he with? What was his past relationship with Paul? With Onesimus?

c. Who is Onesimus? How do you suppose he encountered Paul? What has happened to him since he met Paul?

4. Respond personally to what you see.

a. Imagine yourself as Onesimus. Remember that in the first century runaway slaves were often tortured, maimed, or killed in order to discourage other runaways. How would you be feeling when Paul asked you to go back to your master?

b. Would you go back? Why? Why do you suppose Onesimus went back?

c. Picture yourself as Onesimus peering over Paul's shoulder as he writes this letter. How do you feel about the way Paul is handling the situation? Do you wish that he'd be more firm?

5. A thought to ponder. "Onesimus's return to Philemon was an act of faith in God as was Daniel's walk into the lion's den." Have you ever had to make a similar decision? Where is God now calling you to act boldly for him?

6. Read verses 15-22. Give immediate answers to these questions without a lot of pondering.
   a. Is there anything here that you don't understand? What needs clarification?
   b. What is Paul saying here?
   c. What new insights or thoughts strike you?

7. Take a moment to consider Philemon's dilemma.
   a. As a first-century slave owner he knows that discipline is vital when it concerns a runaway. How can he maintain order with his slaves and yet still fulfill the call of a Christian to be gracious and forgiving?
   b. If he accepts Onesimus without punishment because of his conversion won't other runaways plead conversion upon capture?
   c. How do you suppose the other slave owners would react if Philemon took back Onesimus because he had become a Christian?

8. Respond personally to what you see.
   a. Imagine yourself as Philemon. How would you feel about doing what Paul asks of you?
   b. If you were Philemon, after reading the letter, what would your first words to Onesimus be?

9. A thought to ponder: "The Christian life is a costly life." How was this true for Philemon? How is this true for you?